Eyes of the Heart

Dear Mo —
May your
eyes of your generous
heart ever keep
opening — + your
pens + paint
brushes as well!
Happy Graduation,
+ much love —
Sherry

Eyes of the Heart

Seeking a Path for the Poor
in the Age of Globalization

Jean-Bertrand Aristide

Edited by Laura Flynn

Common Courage Press   Monroe, ME

Library of Congress Cataloging-in-Publication Data

Aristide, Jean-Bertrand.
  Eyes of the heart : seeking a path for the poor in the
age of globalization / Jean-Bertrand Aristide ; edited by
Laura Flynn.
    p. cm.
  Includes index.
  ISBN 1-56751-187-2 -- ISBN 1-56751-186-4 (paper)
    1. Poverty--Haiti. 2. Haiti-Economic conditions--
1971- 3. Globalization. I. Flynn, Laura. II. Title.

HC153.Z9 P613 2000
330.97294'073--dc21

                                          99-086828

Common Courage Press
Box 702
Monroe, ME 04951

(207) 525-0900 fax: (207) 525-3068
orders-info@commoncouragepress.com

www.commoncouragepress.com

First Printing

Contents

Photo by Jennifer Cheek Pantaléon

Preface

Every day I receive letters from my countrymen and -women, hundreds and hundreds of letters. They arrive at my house and at the Foundation, and when I go out the people shower me with their letters. They speak of hardship: the need for a job, a place to live, money to send a child to school, money to feed a child, money to bury a child. Who writes these letters? In Haiti, 85% of the people cannot read or write, so often it is not the sender who puts the words to paper. A mother asks a son to write, a neighbor pays a friend. Further, I know that many of them have to borrow the money to buy the paper and the envelope. These are private letters addressing public issues. The issues are linked to international factors. The people write to me with the hope that I can solve their problems. But since neither the problems nor the solutions begin and end in Haiti, I feel I should forward some of the contents outside of Haiti.

These pages are then written for them, my brothers and sisters in Haiti who cannot write. I write with love and gratitude, born of the deep communion that we share. I forward to you a piece of what the poor of Haiti have taught me. If you are holding this book in your hand, you probably had the opportunity to go to school. Perhaps you are still willing to listen to those who have not; perhaps you are still open to learn. Perhaps you already know something about Haiti, or about other countries facing economic hardship, and you are searching to understand more. Through this letter we would like to open a window for you, a window through which you may see something that touches your own life.

When I see my people there is a question that always arises. How can they survive with so little? How do they create hope where there is no hope? How do they create a way where there is no way? This way that the poor are creating, where there is apparently no way, is what we call the third way. If in the dawn of a new century billions of human beings in poor countries and rich ones alike are dealing with the consequences of economic globalization, we offer this letter as a small contribution to opening a path for the poor in the age of globalization.

Not every letter I receive tells a tale of trouble. I also receive letters of thanks and congratulations, letters thankful for the restoration of democracy in 1994, the end of the repression of the coup period and the disbanding of the Haitian military in 1995. Since the restoration of democracy to Haiti neither began nor ended in Haiti, these thanks must also be shared. On behalf of the Haitian people, I extend again our profound gratitude to all of our friends outside Haiti who have supported our struggle through the years, and particularly to all of those who mobilized, pressured and worked to make the restoration of democracy in 1994 a reality.

Photo by Jennifer Cheek Pantaléon

Chapter One

A Crisis of Faith

Our planet is entering the new century with fully 1.3 billion people living on less than one dollar a day. Three billion people, or half the population of the world, live on less than two dollars a day. Yet this same planet is experiencing unprecedented economic growth. The statistics that describe the accumulation of wealth in the world are mind-boggling. From where we sit, the most staggering statistics of all are those that reflect the polarization of this wealth. In 1960 the richest 20% of the world's population had 70% of the world's wealth, today they have 86% of the wealth. In 1960 the poorest 20% of the world's population had just 2.3% of the wealth of the world. Today this has shrunk to just barely 1%.

Imagine that the five fingers of your hand represent the world's population. The hand has $100 to share. Today the thumb, representing the richest 20% of the world's population has $86 for itself. The little finger has just $1. The thumb is accumulating wealth with breath-taking speed and never looking back. The little finger is sinking deeper into economic misery. The distance between them grows larger every day.

Behind this crisis of dollars there is a human crisis: among the poor, immeasurable human suffering; among the others, the powerful, the policy makers, a poverty of spirit which has made a religion of the market and its invisible hand. A crisis of imagination so profound that the only measure of value is profit, the only measure of human progress is economic growth.

We have not reached the consensus that to eat is a basic human right. This is an ethical crisis. This is a crisis of faith.

Global capitalism becomes a machine devouring our planet. The little finger, the men and women of the poorest 20%, are reduced to cogs in this machine, the bottom rung in global production, valued only as cheap labor, otherwise altogether disposable. The machine cannot and does not measure their suffering. The machine also does not measure the suffering of our planet. Every second an area the size of a soccer field is deforested. This fact alone should be mobilizing men and women to protect their most basic interest—oxygen. But the machine overwhelms us. The distance between the thumb and the little finger stretches to the breaking point.

Photo by Nicole Toutounji. UNICEF/94-0378

Chapter Two

Globalization

A Choice Between Death and Death

A morgue worker is preparing to dispose of a dozen corpses. One living soul lifts himself off of the table, shakes his head and declares, "I am not dead!" To which the morgue worker answers, "Yes you are. The doctors say that you are dead, so lie down."

In today's global marketplace trillions of dollars are traded each day via a vast network of computers. In this market no one talks, no one touches. Only numbers count.

And yet today this faceless economy is already five times larger than the real, or productive, economy.

We know other market places. On a plain high in the mountains of Haiti, one day a week thousands of people still gather. This is the marketplace of my childhood in the mountains above *Port Salut*. The sights and the smells and the noise and the color overwhelm you. Everyone comes. If you don't come you will miss everything. The donkeys tied and waiting in the woods number in the thousands. Goods are displayed in every direction: onions, leeks, corn, beans, yams, cabbage, cassava, and avocados, mangoes and every tropical fruit, chickens, pigs, goats, and batteries, and tennis shoes, too. People trade goods, and news. This is the center; social, political and economic life roll together. A woman teases and coaxes her client. "*Cherie*, the onions are sweet and waiting just for you." The client laughs and teases back until they make a deal. They share trade, and laughter, gossip, politics, and medical and child-rearing tips. A market exchange, and a human exchange.

We are not against trade, we are not against free trade, but our fear is that the global market intends to annihilate our markets. We will be pushed to the cities, to eat food grown on factory farms in distant countries, food whose price depends on the daily numbers game of the first market. "This is more efficient," the economists say. "Your market, your way of life, is not efficient," they say. But we ask, "What is left when you reduce trade to numbers, when you erase all that is human?"

Globalization, the integration of world markets, has promised to "lift all boats", rich and poor, to bring a global culture of entertainment and consumer goods to everyone—the promise of material

Photo by Alan Pogue

happiness. And indeed, since 1980 most third world countries have embraced globalization. They have opened their economies to the world, lowered tariffs, embraced free trade, and allowed goods and services from the industrialized world to flow in. It seems the world is brought closer together. In fact the gap between the thumb and the little finger has never been larger.

What happens to poor countries when they embrace free trade? In Haiti in 1986 we imported just 7000 tons of rice, the main staple food of the country. The vast majority was grown in Haiti. In the late 1980s Haiti complied with free trade policies advocated by the international lending agencies and lifted tariffs on rice imports. Cheaper rice immediately flooded in from the United States where the rice industry is subsidized. In fact the liberalization of

11

Haiti's market coincided with the 1985 Farm Bill in the United States which increased subsidies to the rice industry so that 40% of U.S. rice growers' profits came from the government by 1987. Haiti's peasant farmers could not possibly compete. By 1996 Haiti was importing 196,000 tons of foreign rice at the cost of $100 million a year. Haitian rice production became negligible. Once the dependence on foreign rice was complete, import prices began to rise, leaving Haiti's population, particularly the urban poor, completely at the whim of rising world grain prices. And the prices continue to rise.

What lessons do we learn? For poor countries free trade is not so free, or so fair. Haiti, under intense pressure from the international lending institutions, stopped protecting its domestic agriculture while subsidies to the U.S. rice industry increased. A hungry nation became hungrier.

In a globalized economy, foreign investment is trumpeted as the key to alleviating poverty. But in fact, the top beneficiary of foreign investment from 1985–95 was the United States, with $477 billion. Britain ran a distant second at $199 billion, and Mexico, the only third world country in the top ten, received only $44 billion in investment. When the majority of this money fled the country overnight during Mexico's financial meltdown in 1995, we learned that foreign investment is not really investment. It is more like speculation. And in my country, Haiti, it's very hard to find investment statistics.

We are still moving from misery to poverty with dignity.

Many in the first world imagine the amount of money spent on aid to developing countries is massive. In fact, it amounts to only .03 % of GNP of the industrialized nations. In 1995, the director of the U.S. aid agency defended his agency by testifying to his congress that 84 cents of every dollar of aid goes back into the U.S. economy in goods and services purchased. For every dollar the United States puts into the World Bank, an estimated $2 actually goes into the U.S. economy in goods and services. Meanwhile in 1995, severely indebted low-income countries paid one billion dollars more in debt and interest to the International Monetary Fund (IMF) than they received from it. For the 46 countries of Subsaharan Africa, foreign debt service was four times their combined governmental health and education budgets in 1996. So, we find that aid does not aid.

The little finger knows that she is sinking deeper into misery each day, but all the while the thumb is telling her that profits are increasing, economies are growing and he is pouring millions of dollars of aid into her country. Whose profit? Whose economy? What aid? The logic of global capitalism is not logical for her. We call this economic schizophrenia.

The history of the eradication of the Haitian Creole pig population in the 1980s is a classic parable of globalization. Haiti's small, black, Creole pigs were at the heart of the peasant economy. An extremely hearty breed, well adapted to Haiti's climate and conditions, they ate readily-available waste products, and could survive for three days without food. Eighty to 85% of rural households raised pigs; they played a key role in maintaining the fertility of the soil and constituted the primary savings bank of the peasant population. Traditionally a pig was sold to pay for emergencies and special occasions (funerals, marriages, baptisms, illnesses and, critically, to pay school fees and buy books for the children when school opened each year in October.)

In 1982 international agencies assured Haiti's peasants their pigs were sick and had to be killed (so that the illness would not spread to countries to the North). Promises were made that better pigs would replace the sick pigs. With an efficiency not since seen among development projects, all of the Creole pigs were killed over period of a thirteen months.

Two years later the new, better pigs came from Iowa. They were so much better that they required clean drinking water (unavailable to 80% of the Haitian population), imported feed (costing $90 a year when the per capita income was about $130), and special roofed pigpens. Haitian peasants quickly dubbed them "*prince à quatre pieds*," (four-footed princes). Adding insult to injury, the meat did not taste as good. Needless to say, the repopulation program was a complete failure. One observer of the process estimated that in monetary terms Haitian peasants lost $600 million dollars. There was a 30% drop in enrollment in rural schools, there was a dramatic decline in the protein consumption in rural Haiti, a devastating decapitalization of the peasant economy and an incalculable negative impact on Haiti's soil and agricultural productivity. The Haitian peasantry has not recovered to this day.

Most of rural Haiti is still isolated from global markets, so for many peasants the extermination of the Creole pigs was their first experience of globalization. The experience looms large in the collective memory. Today, when the peasants are told that "economic reform" and privatization will benefit them they are understandably wary. The state-owned enterprises are sick, we are told, and they must be privatized. The peasants shake their heads and remember the Creole pigs.

The 1997 sale of the state-owned flour mill confirmed their skepticism. The mill sold for a mere $9 million, while estimates place potential yearly profits at $20–30 million a year. The mill was bought by a group of investors linked to one of Haiti's largest banks. One outcome seems certain; this sale will further concentrate wealth—in a country where 1% of the population already holds 45% of the wealth of the country.

If we have lingering doubts about where poor countries fall in this "new" economic order, listen to the World Bank. In September 1996, the *London Guardian* cited a draft World Bank strategy paper that predicted that the majority of Haitian peasants—who make up 70% of Haiti's population—are unlikely to survive bank-advocated free market measures. The Bank concluded: "The small volume of production and the environmental resource constraints will leave the rural population with only two possibilities: to work in the industrial or service sector, or to emigrate." At present the industrial sector employs only about 20,000 Haitians. There are already approximately 2.5 million people living in *Port-au-Prince*, 70% of them are officially unemployed and living in perhaps the most desperate conditions in the Western Hemisphere. Given the tragic history of Haiti's boat people, emigration, the second possibility, can hardly be considered a real option.

The choices that globalization offers the poor remind me of a story. Anatole, one of the boys who had lived with us at *Lafanmi Selavi**, was working at the national port. One day a very powerful businessman offered him money to sabotage the main unloading forklift at the port. Anatole said to the man, "Well, then I am already dead." The man, surprised by the response, asked, "Why?" Anatole answered, "because if I sneak in here at night and do what you ask they will shoot me, and if I don't, you will kill me." The dilemma is, I believe, the classic dilemma of the poor; a choice between death and death. Either we enter a global economic system, in which we know we cannot survive, or, we refuse, and face death by slow starvation. With choices like these the urgency of finding a third way is clear. We

---

* *Lafanmi Selavi* is the center for street children in *Port-au-Prince* founded by Aristide in 1986.

must find some room to maneuver, some open space simply to survive. We must lift ourselves up off the morgue table and tell the experts we are not yet dead.

Photo by Jennifer Cheek Pantaléon

Chapter Three

A Third Way

Another story. On weekends we invite kids from the neighborhood to spend time with us at home. One day, Florence, a beautiful little girl four years old, who has no mother and no father, was visiting. As the kids were preparing to go to swim, I asked Florence where she was going to swim. Florence, who had never seen a pool before, pointed to the pool, and said, "In that big bucket." I asked her if the pool was big or small. And she answered, "It is beautiful." Later as we served the kids cola, I teased her, telling her not to taste it because it was rum. She said, "No, it is cola." I said, "No, Florence, be careful—it is rum." She insisted, "It is cola." I asked her which she preferred—cola or rum? She responded firmly, "I prefer juice." You can imagine how we laughed.

When I presented two options, big or small, she created a third one. When I asked which she preferred, rum or cola, again Florence created a third choice. Florence is a child responding in a spontaneous way. But we adults thinking rationally—can't we do the same? When presented with only two options, we can create a third way.

The poor have long experience in creating a third way. They face death and death every day. They survive. In Haiti we have survived for hundreds of years this way. This may be a jarring notion for those who believe the poor are poor because they are stupid. If one believes this, one will always feel that the solution to poverty will not come from those who are poor. But in fact, if we are alive at all it is not because of aid or help from other countries, rather despite it. We are alive because of our tremendous capacity for survival. The experience of the poor, not only in Haiti, but around the world, is a kind of museum of humanity.

The average Haitian survives on less than 250 U.S. dollars a year. This requires imagination every day. One percent of the population controls 45% of the national wealth. There is no welfare. In *Cite Soleil, Port-au-Prince*'s largest slum, 400,000 people live in 2.5 square miles, in perhaps the worst living conditions in the Western Hemisphere. When you go there you have the impression that the people never sleep; there is activity day and night. This is because there is not enough physical space for everyone to lie down at the same time. They sleep by turns. What sustains these people?

Consider this: Last year a one-month-old baby was found in a pile of garbage by one of our teachers. Ants had eaten part of the child's hand. The teacher, Rose, is a poor woman. She already has two children. Yet she spontaneously adopted the baby, naming him *Ti Moise* (Little Moses). This woman teaches that beyond market values there are human values. That no child can be thrown away.

How do these people survive? Why is suicide practically unheard of in Haiti? To understand we must move beyond statistics. To see the richness of the Haitian people we must examine cultural factors: wealth of humor, warmth of character, ease of laughter, dignity, solidarity. We have traditions in Haiti that allow us to share food when we can. We raise the child of a friend or relative who cannot. We work together in a *Konbit* to bring in a crop, or build a neighbor's house in exchange for a meal shared at the end of the day. We can make one more place on a *tap-tap** that is already impossibly full. The majority of Haitians survive in a vast informal economy that remains beyond the statisticians, yet provides sustenance for 70% of the urban workforce. And then we still smile, and we still laugh. In Haiti we are rich in these. There is a wealth of spirit here and from it a third way emerges.

One day, not too long ago, two European sailors docked on Haitian shores for the first time. Like Columbus, their maps were not accurate. Their book of Caribbean ports told them there was a harbor at *Ibo Lele* beach—a small island in the bay of *Port-au-Prince*. They imagined that once finished with immi-

---

* A *tap-tap* is a covered pick-up truck that serves as public transportation in *Port-au-Prince*.

gration and port formalities they would eat at a restaurant and then call the friend in *Port-au-Prince* whom they had come to visit. When they arrived there was no port, no restaurant, no telephone, no coast guard, and no official to record their arrival, just a dilapidated peer and an abandoned hotel. On the beach fisherman were quietly pulling their boats to shore. After a time one of the fishermen approached and offered them a ride to the mainland. Another offered to watch their boat. On shore, one person after another offered to help the lost *blan* find their way. These "boat people" were well received. Finally, they were led to a distant working telephone where they could call their friend. The experience made a deep impression. They had traveled many places, they said, but Haiti felt different. From the moment they arrived they felt something magic. What the country lacked in amenities the people made up for in hospitality. Misery has not destroyed the hospitality of the people. When Columbus landed on our island he was welcomed with open arms by the Arawak Indians. Our island still welcomes visitors with open arms, only now we keep our eyes open, too.

In Haiti we also mobilize. We have been mobilizing throughout our history. We mobilized to end a thirty-year dictatorship. We mobilized in Haiti and in the Haitian Diaspora throughout the three years of the *coup d'etat*. Haiti has nine geographic departments; we call the over 1 million Haitians living outside of Haiti the tenth department. During the coup period, Haitians demonstrated every day through the freezing winters in Canada and the United States. I should add that this same tenth department mobilizes economically for Haiti every day. Each year they send between $400 and $600 million back to family in Haiti. This solidarity represents the powerful bank of human and financial resources Haiti has in its Diaspora. We know that mobilizing these resources for Haiti's development will be one of the keys to our future.

On September 30, 1998, to mark the seventh anniversary of the *coup d'etat*, we mobilized at my old church *St. Jean Bosco* in *La Saline*. Even before I reached the church the people took me. They led me through *La Saline*, *Saint Martin* and to *Cite Soleil*. The crowd moved and I was swept along. The crowd was so tight around me that I did not know when I had left the church and moved into the streets. (Since the massacre in 1988 the church has walls but no roof—it has yet to be rebuilt.) There were thousands and thousands coming out of their homes to walk with us, lining the streets, standing on roofs. By the time we reached *Cite Soleil*, the number was estimated at 50,000. It was a spontaneous manifestation of hope. When I look in their eyes I see it. Equal measures of desperation and hope. Their eyes tell me they will not sit home and wait. They say if we must die in the streets we will die in the streets. At home we are hungry. But if we sit home we will surely die. If we go to the street we may also die, but there at least there is a glimmer of hope.

In *Cite Soleil* that day the people turned against a local police officer. He was universally disliked and the people said he had murdered residents of the neighborhood. The crowd threatened him and to prevent violence I took the responsibility to protect him. He got out safely. Later he was jailed. I do not know if he will be effectively prosecuted or punished by a justice system that still does not give justice, but one thing is clear—he can never go back to *Cite Soleil*. When we mobilize the people we risk being accused of causing riots, of fomenting violence, of campaigning. But, if we don't mobilize, the risks are greater.

Let us mobilize for peace in a collective way rather than let the anger, the frustration and the helplessness explode in violence. Between the death of resignation and the death of violent explosion, collective mobilization is a third way. It is an indispensable concentration of human energy. There will never be money enough, but there are people enough.

The third way for which we are searching is not something new. It is not something we will have to invent. A wealth of experience, knowledge, skill, energy and the power to mobilize resides with the poor. From this creativity, this panorama of human endurance of the poor in Haiti, and the poor in Mexico, and in Brazil, and Southeast Asia and Africa, and more and more of the poor in North America and Europe, we can learn.

Photo by Jennifer Cheek Pantaléon

Chapter Four

"Give Me Chocolate!"

Officially, slavery no longer exists in Haiti. But through the lives of children in Haiti who live as "*restaveks*" we see the remnants of slavery. *Restaveks* are children, usually girls, sometimes as young as 3 and 4 years old, who live in the majority of Haitian families as unpaid domestic workers. They are the first to get up in the morning and the last to go to bed at night. They carry water, clean house, do errands and receive no salary. Often they are from the countryside; their parents send them to the city in the hope that the family they live with will give them food and send them to school. The family that takes in the *restavek* is more often than not just one rung up on the economic ladder. Most families struggle to send their own children to school—let alone the *restavek*. So most often *restavek* children are not in school; they eat what is left when the others are finished, and they are extremely vulnerable to verbal, physical and sexual abuse.

Officially, Haiti is a free country. But through the economic life of the country we see the remnants of colonialism. Ours is an economy of dependence, a *restavek* economy. Because of foreign food imports our agricultural production has fallen to historic lows. Because we export little our currency is weak. Haitian workers earn the lowest wages in the hemisphere. We are encouraged to exploit and maintain this so-called advantage to attract foreign companies to come. Because our economy is weak we depend on loans and aid from foreign countries to support our national budget. This makes us extremely vulnerable to pressure from international institutions that control the money.

Bertony was a *restavek* when we met him. He came to the house with a group of children from our neighborhood to spend the day. He was five years old. That day Bertony played, swam and ate all he wanted. When he went home he bragged to the children of the family with whom he lived about this rare day. When the parents heard, they were angry. They would not stand to have this little *restavek* teasing their own children who had not enjoyed such privilege. They threw Bertony out, saying that if he was such a big man he should go back to Aristide's house. Bertony had broken the first rule of the *restavek*. The *restavek* has no right to speak. Fortunately Bertony, being a very clever boy, found his way to *Lafanmi Selavi*, where he quickly became integrated into the life of the house, going to school and working at the kids' radio station. Today 7-year-old Bertony is a journalist at *Radyo Timoun*. He not only speaks; the whole country hears him.

One day two Americans were giving an English lesson. They had the kids repeat a simple phrase,

Photo by Jennifer Cheek Pantaléon

"Give me water." When the children answered correctly they were given chocolate. When they called on Bertony he responded, "Give me chocolate." They asked him, "Why don't you say give me water." He replied, "Who told you I was thirsty?"

Haiti, Latin America's oldest republic, was not always poor. In 1789 it was France's most valuable colony and accounted for one-third of all French commerce. Haiti produced 60% of the world's coffee. More ships docked in our ports than in the great trading center of Marseilles. And in that same year, Haiti produced more wealth than all thirteen of the North American colonies put together.

In 1791, our ancestors, the producers of this great wealth, revolted against servitude in what became the world's only successful slave revolution. The

French waged a total war, which lasted thirteen years, killed hundreds of thousands of Haitians and destroyed Haiti's infrastructure and agricultural productivity. Lasting peace with France was only achieved in 1823 when Haiti agreed to pay 150 million francs to reimburse the French. To pay for our freedom we were forced to mortgage our future. To pay the first 30 million francs, Haitian President Boyer closed all of Haiti's schools, an early case of structural adjustment.

In 1994, when I returned to Haiti after three years in exile, many people felt we were being forced to make a similar compromise. In order to restore democracy we were asked to agree to an economic plan which could once again mortgage the future of the country. At the end of the coup, Haiti's economy was in desperate shape. The economy had shrunk by 30%. Prices of products of primary consumption had increased five-fold during the three years. Government coffers had been completely raided by the coup leaders. International donors conditioned their support on an economic plan following neo-liberal lines: lowered tariffs, tight monetary control and, most prominently, privatization. In August of 1994, two months before I returned to Haiti, I sent a team of economic advisors to a meeting of the international donor agencies in Paris to present a proposed economic plan. The "Paris plan", was never a signed agreement, rather it was a strategy paper. It included many of the elements that the international community was pressing as conditions for financial support of Haiti.

The plan also included other aspects: money for literacy, education, reparations for victims of the coup, and a program for modernization of the state-owned enterprises with built-in safeguards to ensure that the end result was not a further polarization of the already grotesque distribution of wealth in Haiti. We tried to be pragmatic regarding the state enterprises. We knew that the Haitian state did not have the money needed to invest to provide services to all of Haiti's people. But we also wanted to guard against a quick total sale of state assets. The size of shares of companies bought was to be small enough to allow middle-class or Diaspora Haitians to participate, ten percent ownership of the state enterprises was to be reserved as reparations for victims of the coup.

There is a Haitian proverb that goes, *"Tankou wozo nou pliye, men nou pa kase."* "Like reeds, we bend but do not break." The way of the reeds is a third way as well. Given the circumstances of the time, the Paris plan fit this strategy. We compromised where we had to, but held fast on the issues we felt were most important to the vast majority of the people. Unfortunately, even this compromise was too progressive for some elements in the international community and for some in Haiti. So by September of 1995 the IMF was insisting on a new stand-by agreement, which included all the structural adjustment provisions and none of the progressive programs or guarantees of the Paris plan. I refused.

Behind the scenes hands were moving too quickly and quietly to sell the flour and cement mills without parliamentary approval, in direct contradiction to the Haitian constitution. On September 30, 1995, in an interview with national radio and television from the palace, I said, "If anyone dares to violate the law of the republic in selling one of these state enterprises, he or she will be immediately arrested." The prime minister resigned. Powerful voices in the international community made a lot of noise about "cutting off all funds to Haiti." The international media followed suit with a frenzy of condemnation. Once again the propaganda machine ignited the fire of character assassination. Once again the psychological pressure campaign began. However, over a decade of experience means that we are used to this.

Just a few months earlier, the president of the World Bank had visited Haiti. After discussing economic issues we had taken an unplanned walking tour through *La Saline*, one of the poorest areas of *Port-au-Prince*, where I worked as a priest in the 1980s. There, to complement what we had discussed, he had an opportunity to see with his own eyes the reality we face. Does this mean we were playing on emotional chords? No. Sometimes it is necessary to compare what you hear with what you see. Without doubt all those who participated in this tour came away with a clearer picture of Haiti.

The IMF stand-by agreement we were being asked to sign contained conditions we could not accept, conditions we knew would only deepen the poverty of the country. Is this the goal of the IMF or the World Bank? They would say no. We must hold them to their word on this and negotiate accordingly. We know what they saw in *La Saline*. They saw what we already knew. If alleviation of this poverty is really our mutual goal, that trip through *La Saline* fortified Haiti's negotiating position.

In November we formed a new government with the first woman prime minister in Haiti's history. We submitted a new stand-by letter, which placed the alleviation of poverty as its primary focus, while calling for a continued national debate on the economic program. The World Bank was the first to welcome this alternative—perhaps the trip through *La Saline* helped. Afterwards, the rest of the international community also accepted the letter. The victory was, of course, short lived. A few months later, after I left the presidency; a new government was in place, which took a different course. But the lesson, I believe, is that there is room for negotiation, even when the balance of power seems so uneven. We should never forget that international lending institutions need us, as we need them. They are lending us money, not giving it to us. This is business, not charity. Only by defending our interests will we cease to be a *restavek* state, in perpetual economic dependence. When they offer us water, it is our right and our responsibility to ask for chocolate.

Photo by Jennifer Cheek Pantaléon

Chapter Five

Democratizing Democracy

I n nations around the world, even those experiencing rapid economic growth, there are millions of children living on the streets, refugees of a system that puts the market before the person. If we listen closely, these children have a message for the new century. Thirteen years ago we opened a center for street children in *Port-au-Prince*. In 1996, we opened a radio station with our 400 kids. *Radyo Timoun* (Little People's Radio) broadcasts their music, their news, and their commentaries 14 hours a day. In a world in which a child under the age of 5 dies every 3 seconds, children must speak. In a commentary on democracy prepared by three eleven-year-old girls, democracy was defined as food, school, and health care for everyone. Simplistic or visionary? For them democracy in Haiti doesn't mean a thing unless the people can eat.

Democracy asks us to put the needs and rights of people at the center of our endeavors. This means investing in people. Investing in people means first of all food, clean water, education and healthcare.

These are basic human rights. It is the challenge of any real democracy to guarantee them.

Ironically, in many countries of the South the transition to democracy comes at a time when states are being forced to rapidly divest of resources, saddled with debt, abandoning the economic field to market forces, and playing a smaller and smaller role in the provision of basic human services. They have neither the money nor the will to invest in their people. Today democracy risks being rapidly outpaced by the galloping global economy. If democracy in rich countries and poor ones alike is to be more than a façade, nice in theory, but irrelevant in the face of global economic relationships, our concept and practice of democracy must make a giant leap forward. We must democratize democracy.

Do not confuse democracy with the holding of elections every four or five years. Elections are the exam, testing the health of our system. Voter participation is the grade. But school is in session every day. Only the day-to-day participation of the people at all levels of governance can breathe life into democracy and create the possibility for people to play a significant role in shaping the state and the society that they want.

I recently heard a beautiful story about holding representatives accountable in democracy. In Columbia a member of an indigenous community was elected to parliament to represent his people. On one particularly important vote, the community elders had decided how they wished their representative to vote. The parliamentarian, now far away from his community in the halls of power in the capital, voted differently. Again the elders met and agreed that for defying the wishes of the community he was elected to represent, the parliamentarian should walk many miles through the mountains and then bathe in the freezing water of a sacred mountain lake in order to purge himself. This he did, and balance within the community was restored. Perhaps this technique would not be appropriate elsewhere, but the point is that it is up to each country and indeed each community to search for ways to both keep the peace and protect against the potential betrayal of elected leaders.

The governed must build new relationships with the governors. When decisions are made for the people and without the people they are often made against the people.

Civil society plays a critical role in democratizing democracy. We in Haiti are creating spaces for democratic participation. A radio station run by street children is one. Our foundation is another. The Aristide Foundation for Democracy is a place where rich and poor can discuss and debate national and international issues. The people meet here to talk about *lavichè* (the high cost of living), Haiti's international debt, about education and literacy, justice and health care.

We are mobilizing for peace with the slogan, "*Pa gen lape nan tet, si pa gen lape nan vant*," "there is no peace in the head if there is no peace in the stomach." In a country like Haiti, words alone are not enough. It would be hypocritical to offer hungry people only food, and never let them talk. Likewise it is demagoguery to offer them only words. Political participation is meaningless without economic participation. So while the Foundation is a place of dialogue, it is also a place of action, where we are creating structures for economic participation. In 1996, we created a cooperative economic structure that now includes 13,000 people. The members are street vendors, shoe shiners, day laborers, the poorest of the poor. The majority are women. The cooperative offers the following services to its members:

1) Credit at low interest rates. (1% a month vs. 20–100% elsewhere.)
2) A community store offering basic necessities, rice, beans, cooking oil, flour, sugar, etc. at about two-thirds of market prices.
3) A transportation branch which offers public transport in *Port-au-Prince* to members at only a percentage of the normal fares.
4) Investment in cooperative agricultural projects to encourage food production in Haiti.

The keystone of our work at the Foundation is respect for traditional strategies of survival among the poor. In Haiti the poor have a collective tradition for saving money called *sôld* or *men*, which means "hands put together." Each person in a group puts a small amount of money into a pot every day or every week. Every week a different member of the group gets the pot. Our cooperative builds on this tradition, by lending to people in groups on a rotating basis. This is economics with a human face.

The people we work with are the *marchan dlo* and *marchan fresko*, women hawking water and sodas for a few gourdes in the streets; the *bayakou* who clean latrines at night; the shoe shiners who labor in the hot sun each day; the *bouretye*, who pull impossibly heavy carts through the crowded streets of *Port-au-Prince*. This is Haiti. These are the people who form our vast and vibrant "informal" sector.

Around the world what is called the informal sector makes up a $16 trillion-a-year economy. Of this women are responsible for $11 trillion. In Haiti, where official unemployment is about 70%, the informal sector is in fact much larger than the formal sector. And the economic strength of this sector in Haiti is a surprise to most economists. It has a total combined asset and property value estimated at $4.71 billion, or more than 72% of the total assets and property of the 123 largest private enterprises in Haiti. It is a complex network of economic activities that extends into every Haitian villages and percolates through the urban slums, touching the lives of the rural and urban poor majority. Any economic plan for Haiti must begin here.

Any economic plan for Haiti must also begin with women. In Haiti we say that women are the *poto mitan*, or "center pole" of the household. During the past 20 years we can say that women have also

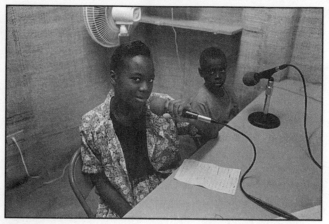

Photo by Alan Pogue

been the *poto mitan* of the struggle. We are not surprised then when we see that over 70% of the members of our Foundation are women. As at *St. Jean Bosco*, the majority of those who attended were women. In the struggle women are always well represented at the bases, if not in positions of power.

Women have unique skills for leadership with cooperation. When we created the cooperative at the Foundation we took some inspiration from the Grameen Bank in Bangladesh. We decided to lend money to people in groups of five, with each member being responsible for the others. The women understood and adapted to the system quickly. Many of the men balked. It was not easy to find four others with whom they could form a group, and when it came time to make a loan they did not want to sign for the others.

Studies around the world have shown that when household budgets are in the hands of women, they are more likely to be spent for primary needs (food, education, and health care). I predict that when the budgets of nations are in the hands of women we will see the same result. While I was president, women held major cabinet posts for the first time in Haiti. We had fifteen women ministers in three governments, including a Prime Minister, Minster of Foreign Affairs and Ministers of Finance, Education, Information and Labor. It made a difference.

Women, children and the poor must be the subjects, not the objects of history. They must sit at the decision-making tables and fill the halls of power. They must occupy the radio and airwaves, talking to and calling to account their elected leaders. Their participation will democratize democracy, bringing the word back to its full meaning: *Demos* meaning people, *Cratei* meaning to govern.

Photo by Jennifer Cheek Pantaléon

Chapter Six

The Water of Life

On weekends it is the kids from *Lafanmi Selavi* who come to our house to spend time, to share food, talk, play and swim in the swimming pool. It is a small pool, too small for four hundred kids, but for them it is a piece of paradise. Sometimes we invite other children; *restaveks*, children from parishes in *Port-au-Prince*; sometimes a *Lafanmi Selavi* bus goes to *Cite Soleil*, to *La Saline*, to *Carrefour* to pick up children who want to swim. This experience, which may appear at first as merely symbolic, has tremendous ramifications. In a country where only 20% of the population have access to clean drinking water, swimming pools are exclusively for the rich. There is not a single public swimming pool in Haiti. The pool itself is a symbol of the elite.

We know the kids need food, we know they need school, but we cannot give all of them these things in a day. So while we are working to change the society, we can give them a day in a swimming pool. We say no child is so poor she does not deserve to swim in a pool. And if you imagine this has no impact on the society, think again.

The kids swim with us, with their teachers, with a group of agronomists who work with them on Saturdays, and with American friends and volunteers working at *Lafanmi Selavi*. A mix of races and social classes in the same water. Sometimes these images have appeared on television. Shortly after we began this experience we started hearing reports from friends among the upper classes of rumors that I was preparing these "*vagabon*," these street children, to invade their swimming pools. Were it not tragic it would be comic. Perhaps the real root of the fear is this: If a maid in a wealthy home sees children from *Cite Soleil* swimming in a swimming pool on television, she may begin to ask why her child cannot swim in the pool of her boss.

So it is a system of social apartheid that we are questioning. We saw the same phenomena during the civil rights movement in the United States where attempts to integrate beaches and swimming pools met with some of the worst violence of the period. The same was true in South Africa. What we are facing in Haiti is a form of apartheid. There are no laws on the books enforcing segregation but the social and economic forces at play are so powerful they create a de facto Apartheid. The polarizations are many: literate/illiterate, rich/poor, black/white, male/female, those who have clean water to drink/those who don't. In Haiti, where these polarities remain so strong, swimming in the same water has both psychological and social repercussions. You swim with people you are close to. If you are a family, if you are a community, swimming together may improve the quality of the relationship. Our experience has shown that the water can help to melt the barriers between us, and wash away the dirt of prejudice.

Another story came to us after the visit of the famous Haitian-American rap group the Fugees. They played a concert for the rich at Haiti's Club Med. The lead singer was once himself a very poor child growing up in *Port-au-Prince*. And he continually reminded the crowd of this. One of the concert goers was heard to say that the singer did not need to keep talking as this would just make the kids in the street "*plis sou moun.*" The closest translation is "they will think they are somebody." Another person, talking about the kids swimming in the pool, said, "If my dog falls in my swimming pool I will clean it. But if one of Aristide's dogs falls in my pool they will be swimming in their own blood."

In 1991, on the first day of my presidency, I invited the poor to breakfast. The palace doors, forever closed to them, were opened. To this day many among the elite feel that the palace has been dirtied by the presence of the poor. At the time the response was the *coup d'etat* which did indeed bathe the country in blood.

How do we wash away the dirt of prejudice? Little by little? With a cleansing flood? With a *lavalas*?

When my daughter was born in 1996, we asked where should we baptize her? In this country of ridged social delineation, the place that we chose would say something about who she is. In the end we choose *Lafanmi Selavi*. There at the house, among the children of the streets, and in the presence of many friends of all social classes, Christine was baptized by her godfather Bishop Willy Romelus. The water of life can baptize us all new. One people, God's children, swimming together in the water of life.

In Haiti's countryside the people are crying out for the water of life, too. The 70% of Haiti's population that lives in the countryside needs water to grow the food that can feed the country. If Haiti is to be economically independent we must be able to feed ourselves. To do that we must heal the land. If we go back for a moment to history we can trace the roots of our current ecological crisis to Haiti's heavy debt to France in the 19th century, which encouraged the logging of Haiti's tropical forests for export to Europe. Today only 3% of our forests remain. Without the trees to hold the soil, 1% of Haiti's topsoil washes to sea each year, driving Haiti's peasant farmers further into poverty as the land produces less and less each year.

Since our independence in 1804, every Haitian government has governed on the backs of the peasants, taxing their produce and giving nothing back in return. A deep chasm between people in the countryside and people in the capital has always existed. This chasm is inscribed in the language. Anyone who lives outside of *Port-au-Prince* is called *moun andeyò*, literally, "outside people," outsiders.

And the language was inscribed in the law. Historically, *paysanne* ("peasant," in French) was listed on the birth certificates of anyone born outside *Port-au-Prince*. When I became president in 1991, by Presidential decree we changed the law, so that now all birth certificates are the same. Now we must keep working to change the language—and the realities of life in the countryside.

On our continent, the banking industry has grown from 40% of the economy to 57% over the last ten years while agriculture has shrunk from 30% to 15% over the same period. In Haiti, agriculture was 50% of our gross national product ten years ago—now it is only 28%. The banks in Haiti extend only 2% of their lending to the agricultural sector. How can we ask the poor, who are mostly peasants, to put their money in these banks?

Article 247 of the Haitian constitution says, "agriculture is the principal wealth of the nation and the guarantee of the well-being of the population." Yes, but where will we find water to irrigate the land? If only 2% of bank lending goes to agriculture, how will the peasants have money to irrigate, to buy water pumps, to buy seeds, to invest in the land?

In the world at large we see this same picture. 3.1 billion people make their living in agriculture. Their lives are on a collision course with globalization. They cannot compete with industrialized western agriculture with its heavy use of pesticides and fertilizers. And yet the world economy is not creating new jobs for them. What will they do?

Peasants are forced off their land, move to over-crowded cities where they find neither jobs nor health care, nor schools for their children, or even clean water to drink. The people follow the land. After the trees are cut from the mountains, the soil washes to the plains, and the people follow. When the soil washes away from the plains, the people once again follow, moving to the slums of cities by the sea.

The economically powerful are not protecting the land, the trees, the soil or the people who have existed on this land for generations. Can we expect that aid programs will help our environment or our people who depend on the land? If 84 cents of every dollar is going back to the donor country, how much is left for water for the peasants? Or for trees to hold the water and the soil? The question is dramatic. What will we do to have water?

We are at the millenium and there is still no water for the people to drink—let alone water for the land. Sometimes foreigners think we are lazy, asking for food, asking for handouts. But in fact we are asking for water. In our rich country, where the sun shines every day, I assure you that if we have water we will grow the food we need to eat.

Some may ask how a strategy of national development based on agriculture can possibly succeed in this day and age, in the face of the macro economic realities we are facing. In fact, we cannot know for sure. But what we can be sure of is that as long as Haitian governments continue to receive instructions from international institutions we will move from the same to the same, the same program to the same program, from bad to worse. On the other side, if we see organizations in Haiti among civil society looking for strategies that come from the people, this represents a candle in the night. Hope in a night of despair. We can offer an alternative. An alternative that will not make us rich, but may at least save us from starvation and lead us to poverty with dignity. If what we propose is not perfect, what they proposed has already demonstrated how disastrous it is.

This is a strategy for subsistence, for survival. And that is just what the poor have always done in the face of macro economic realities that have never been favorable.

The neo-liberal strategy is to weaken the state in order to have the private sector replace the state. Through cooperatives we can perhaps preserve some margin of public services. Without a national mobilization of human resources, we will never be able to create a balance between that economic power and that human power. The human power in my country is the huge majority of the poor. The economic power is that tiny 1% that controls 45% of the wealth.

The *coup d'etat* of 1991 showed how terribly afraid the 1% is of the mobilization of the poor. They are afraid of those under the table—afraid they will see what is on the table. Afraid of those in *Cite Soleil*, that they will become impatient with their own misery. Afraid of the peasants, that they will not be "*moun andeyò*" anymore. They are afraid that those who cannot read will learn how to read. They are afraid that those who speak Creole will learn French, and no longer feel inferior. They are afraid of the poor entering the palace, of the street children swimming in the pool. They are not afraid of me. They are afraid that what I say may help the poor to see.

But in the end, on this small planet, we are all swimming in the same water.

Photo by Jennifer Cheek Pantaléon

Chapter Seven

A Taste of Salt

In Haitian iconography the zombie is one whose soul has been stolen in order to enslave his body to his master. The powerful fear evoked by the fate of the zombie in Haitian consciousness stems from the collective memory of slavery. To wake the zombie, to free his soul, you must give him a taste of salt.

I f for 200 years the Haitian people have not been taught to read and write, it is no accident of history. If there are no schools in the countryside for the sons and daughters of those who work the land, it is no accident. If every literacy campaign has failed to reach great numbers of people, it is no accident. If even in 1991 and again in 1994 when as president I spoke to international donors over and over about the need for adult literacy they looked at me as if I was crazy, it is no accident. If today 85% of the Haitian people cannot read and write, it is no accident.

We live amongst the ruins of a social structure built to separate and divide. And education and language are the pillars of this structure.

Only 15% of the people speak French and yet for 200 years the justice system, the education system, and all government business has been conducted in French, written in French. Land titles, birth certificates, all were written in French.

It is estimated that only half of Haitian children are in school. And only 139 children of every 1000 who enter primary school finish secondary school.

How hungry are the people to learn? How desperate are they to send their children to school?

In Haiti, September and October are difficult months as parents struggle to find the money to send their children to school, or worse, resign themselves once again to not being able. Even in the public schools (which have room for only 10% of the school-age population), parents must buy school books, uniforms and school supplies. This is a monumental task for families barely eating each day. In September of 1998, the Foundation began a new project: selling schoolbooks at half price. When we announced the book sale, we had literally thousands of people—mothers, father and children—lined up from 5:00 A.M. each morning in front of the Foundation. We sold books for two solid weeks— reaching over 10,000 school children—and then extended the project to the countryside—to *Jeremie*, *Gonaives*, *Les Cayes* and *Jacmel*.

If we are to build a new social structure based on inclusion, the minimum foundation must include free education for every child—as promised but not yet delivered by our constitution—and Creole literacy for every adult.

In the Spring of 1998, high school and university students meeting at a conference on education at the Foundation announced, "We who have had the privilege of going to school have a debt to pay to our country. That is why we commit to teaching our parents, our relatives, our neighbors how to read and write." We urged them to proceed with humility, setting their sights initially just on the area where the Foundation is located, because we know the weight of past failure weighs heavy, and we know that we cannot replace the state whose duty it is to educate the people. Still they began. Now two hours a day, five days a week, for six-month sessions, they teach. These young people themselves face uncertain futures, most are barely scratching by, struggling to stay in school, with no certain prospects for jobs even if they are able to finish. And yet they give their time for no pay. Literacy classes take place in the late afternoons, when the participants are done with their work. In the rainy season the rains come in the afternoons. This means that more days than not the young people make their way home in the rain and the dark. Let them inspire us. Let them give force to those who are tired, who have become cynical, who don't believe strategies like these can work in 1999. Young people are excellent at forging third ways.

The young teaching the old is a third way. A university or even high school student in Haiti, though he or she may be poor, is already part of a privileged group. Their education has subtly and not so subtly taught them to separate themselves from those who cannot read, from their own parents, in many cases. So the experience of literacy programs in itself can help to break down separation—help them to come home. As they stand before their elders, they gain new respect. As teachers they are forced to find ways to communicate, and they gain new familiarity with reading and writing their own language, which may have been neglected in school.

And those learning? They are tasting salt. And once they taste it they want more.

But wait a minute, you ask, doesn't he know that Poalo Friere is dead, liberation theology a thing of the history books, and literacy campaigns the stuff of past revolutions?

The people don't seem to think so.

Remember that history moves in waves. We cannot expect to always live on the crests. We have to keep floating even when the waters ebb. And to those who say that liberation theology has failed because it is empty, because it is weak, because it no longer offers a response to the questions we face, I say you may be seriously underestimating the force and power of the machine that sought to crush the theology of love.

The weapons aimed at us today are subtler than the old ones. Haiti was one of the last places on this continent where reactionary forces attempted to use overt violence to silence a people. They failed. Today we face complex networks of communications and disinformation, corporations with budgets hundreds of times the size of our national budget, and an army of international financial, trade, and development institutions. The panorama of threats is so daunting that sometimes I say perhaps our only strength is that the majority of the people **did not** go to school. They are not yet assimilated into this machine. Their minds remain their own and they are experts at unearthing the truth in a morass of disinformation.

The reflections made by peasants are sharp. So sharp that we know the light of liberation burns bright among them. Whole counties once awakened do not go to sleep forever. As once a person tastes the salt, she will never willingly be a slave again.

Up until now, those who go to university are those who govern Haiti. But if the country survives, it is on the strength of those who did not go to university. How intelligent must one be to construct a three-story building without the benefit of a formal education? I know people who have. How intelligent must one be to manage a business with a budget of $300,000 U.S. without being able to read and write? I know people who do. How bright must one be to navigate a small sailboat through "the passage of death"—as the windward channel which separates

Photo by Alan Pogue

Haiti from Cuba is known among Haitian sailors—
and reach Miami, with no maps, no navigational
instruments, no lights...There are thousands who
have done it.

58

In 1988, after they burned *St. Jean Bosco*, my dream was to create a popular university, an educational center that could welcome geniuses like these. We wished both to value the intelligence they already possess and to open doors that have been closed for them until now.

Today through the work of the Foundation and of *Lafanmi Selavi* we are halfway down the road towards creating that university. The children of *Lafanmi Selavi*—street children—work with agronomists learning how to grow food. Market women and other small entrepreneurs are learning how to form cooperative economic structures. At *Radyo Timoun*, young people from all over the country are learning communications, and at the same time they are teaching the whole country that you don't need a university degree to speak on the radio.

What more do we need to complete the university? An experimental farm and environmental study center, a center dedicated to the study and practice of informal sector economics, a faculty of adult literacy—these are among the departments we will add.

A cornerstone principle of this university is that knowledge is not a commodity—it is meant to be shared. For this reason, communications that enable large numbers of people to participate in educational experiences are central to our mission. *Radyo Timoun* is already an on-air popular university—broadcasting primary school classes to a country in which the majority of children are not in school. *Tele Timoun*, an educational children's television station which went on the air in 1999, has the same mission.

The research done at this university will be done on the ground. Social and economic issues will be studied and solutions tried. There is no book that will tell us how to solve the problems of the over 500,000 children in domestic servitude in Haiti. No book will tell us how to offer economic alternatives to the woman who hawks sodas in the streets to support her children. There is no book that will teach us how to keep trees growing on *Morne Kabrit*, or in the northwest of Haiti. We will have to continue to experiment.

Our university may shock some people. That may be good. This shock may help us break down social barriers, which have been impassible for the past two centuries.

Photo by Jennifer Cheek Pantaléon

Chapter Eight

Material Questions, Theological Answers?

Too often we hear of people fighting against one another in the name of God. We say hunger has no religion, exploitation has no religion, injustice has no religion.

What do we mean when we say God? We mean the source of love; we mean the source of justice. We mean woman and man, black and white, child and adult, spirit and body, past and future, that thing which animates all of us. Something that we cannot touch, yet we feel, something that we cannot listen for, yet we hear. Behind the words, whatever words we choose, is a transcendence that is known to all of us.

We begin with what is in front of us. I cannot see God, but I can see you. I cannot see God, but I see the child in front of me, the woman, the man. Through them, through this material world in which we live, we know God. Through them we know and experience love, we glimpse and seek justice.

The kind of struggle in which we are engaged requires a connection to this transcendence. Some may call this faith, some may call it theology, some may call it values, principles, love, justice. The name is not important. What is important is that we have it. In order to struggle we must be on solid rock. This machine we are facing is not a small one. Its arsenal of capital, of words, of logic, seems to be an unstoppable force. If we are not rooted in faith it will overwhelm us. Among the poor we see this so clearly. They would not survive without their faith.

Let us be clear. We are not talking about a motivation or a faith based in fear, in a fear of God. We move from love. And this love gives great power. It is the power that energized our church, *St. Jean Bosco*, and it is the power that today energies our cooperative.

St. Jean Bosco was a place of light. On September 11, 1988, the people came to celebrate the God of love. The thugs came that day to try to extinguish the light of love. They massacred twenty and injured many, many more, in a siege that lasted many hours. And then they set fire to the church. At one point two men pointed their guns at my head. One in front, one behind. I know with certainty that if the power of non-violence, if the power of love, is not stronger than weapons, I would have died that day. Communities of love are powerful. Even if they are temporarily dispersed they are not extinguishable.

In the spring of 1996, we reunited the parishioners of *St. Jean Bosco* at the Foundation. It was a day of painful reflection as we shared memories and relived our Calvary. Yet out of this experience the community was reborn. These people are among the poorest of *Port-au-Prince*, from *La Saline* and *Cite Soleil*. We wanted to confront this economic misery together. We read from the Acts of the Apostles 4:32 where it says that "All those who believed in God had one heart, and they put what they had in common. No one could say that what was his was for him alone." Drawing on this verse we created a cooperative into which each of the 13,000 members put a small amount and from which each in turn is eligible to take small loans. Later the cooperative opened a community store where the members can buy rice, beans, and other necessities for about two-thirds of the market price. The power of this cooperative is not its economic capital—it is the capital of confidence that the members are building. They are investing in one another, something the global economy is unwilling to do.

We are working among a people who believe deeply in God. So we create an approach that does not reject their faith. Our work is rooted in this faith and the faith illuminates the experience. We are building a community of faith. And because of this we can go quickly.

Does faith mean the absence of doubts and questions? No. The struggle is transcendent; it crosses borders of time and place. As the Exodus is transcendent. We are ever crossing the desert, moving from Egypt to the promised land. As they journeyed, the people of Israel questioned Moses, "Why have you led us into this wilderness? We have escaped slavery, but now we are thirsty and starving in this desert. We have fled one death to find another." It is a moment of doubt. As each of us faces times of doubt in our own lives.

For myself, facing the unmet expectations of the Haitian people is a challenge. To be president in a country where so many people are waiting for food and jobs, when you know that you cannot provide them soon—this was a heavy burden. Our economic situation was, and still is, so desperate, that while I was President I often said, "I am feeding the people with words." But not just any words. In such a situation only the truth will feed their faith. After finishing my term as president, I asked them, "I was with you in *St. Jean Bosco*; you were poor. You sent me to the palace; you were poor. I left the Palace and still you are poor. Why do you still listen to me?" Perhaps part of the answer is in this story. One day last year a group of people who had fled Haiti during the coup and then been returned by the U.S. Coast Guard sat in front of the gate to my house asking to see me. I hesitated because I knew they wanted financial help and didn't know what I could offer. I had many, many meetings that day, and finally around 11:00 P.M. when I finished, a security guard came to tell me the refugees were still there. Still not seeing what I could offer, I decided to go to them. One woman was stretched out on the pavement. I leaned down and kissed her on the cheek. She banged her hand on the ground and said, "Tonight this concrete is softer than any box spring mattress because you treat me with dignity and respect."

There will never be enough money to give each person the house, the job, the school fees that they need, but we always have enough humanity to treat one another with the respect and dignity that we all deserve.

People know when they are being treated with respect, as they know when they are being lied to. The people recognize demagogy. *Analphabet pa bet.* "Illiterate but not stupid." It is the same when two friends share sincerity, respect, and honesty. Then in the face of difficulties, even when they do not have the answers, they are not powerless. Communities of love, where truth is shared, have this same power to traverse difficult times.

There is today as there is always a small group working for peace, working for justice. A small group who may say, "The holy spirit is upon me, because he has anointed me to announce the good news to the poor; to proclaim release for the prisoners and recovery of sight for the blind; to set at liberty those who are oppressed."

Armed with our faith, we should not fear doubt, questions or criticism. The thirst and the hunger of those wandering in the wilderness are also signs of life. It is good when those who do not have enough to eat cry out.

And those who are hungry for justice must cry out too. When I returned to Haiti, I knew that the system rooted in corruption would not be able to give justice to the victims. Over 5000 people were killed, thousands more beaten, raped, and imprisoned during the coup.

And the victims had to face the criminals on the streets every day. It was not an easy situation. We said no to retaliation. But we could not bless impunity either. Biblical reconciliation comes after judgment. And I know that Haiti will not be truly reconciled until the victims find justice through the judicial system. This will not come tomorrow. But we continue to work so that it will come.

Lafanmi Selavi was victim to this violence too. Twice the thugs set fire to the house and the criminals have not yet been brought to justice. When the house was burned in 1991, four children were killed. One was a 12-year-old boy named Dominique. He rescued several smaller children from the flames and died trying to save others. Dominique was a hero and I still think of him often. In 1995, a little girl named Monique came to live at *Lafanmi Selavi*. When we asked her where her mother was she told us her mother died on the Neptune, an overloaded ferryboat traveling from *Jeremie* to *Port-au-Prince* that sank in 1992 carrying thousands of people. Her father, her mother and five brothers and sisters all died in the wreck. Monique ran to the bathroom on shore just as the boat was pulling out to sea, and was left behind. One child perished in the flames, one saved from the sea. After she heard her family had died, Monique made her way to *Port-au-Prince* where she lived on the streets for four years. Eventually she made her way to *Lafanmi Selavi*. Today Monique is fifteen years old; she dances beautifully and plays the drums. We know that the innocents are still perishing in the flames of violence, but we do not fall into

Photo by Alan Pogue

the sea of despair because God continually feeds us with miracles of life—and Monique is one.

There are many kinds of hunger. Those who have enough to eat may be crying out from spiritual hunger. During the past few years I have traveled and spoken to groups around the world: to students at dozens of U.S. universities, at conferences in Europe, Latin America and Asia. Each time I address a new group I am struck—the same questions, the same hunger for spirituality, for morality in politics, for a recognition of the humanity and dignity of each of God's beings. In Japan, speaking to a group of university students I said, "When someone is hungry, I am hungry; when someone is suffering, I am suffering." And there, through translation, across culture, I saw the unmistakable flash of recognition in their eyes.

Since 1994, an American friend who has lived in Haiti for many years has been leading foreign visitors on a one-day pilgrimage called the "Stations of the Cross." The groups visit fourteen sites, stations in the cross of Haiti's recent history. Beginning at *St. Jean Bosco*, they travel to *Cite Soleil*, to *Lafanmi Selavi*, to *Fort Dimanche*, the Duvalier prison where over 30,000 Haitians died, to the sites of the assassinations of our martyrs Antoine Izmery, Father Jean-Marie Vincent and Justice Minister Guy Malary. In 1996, we began receiving these groups at the Foundation and at our home at the end of the pilgrimage. These visitors, many from the United States, express this same hunger for spirituality and a humane world. We welcome and are encouraged by their solidarity. We are also encouraged that they see Haiti with different eyes than many foreigners. They see not only the misery, the bad roads, the deforestation, but also the strength and dignity of the people, the beauty of the land, and the richness of the culture.

We call this last stop the 15th station, the station of resurrection. The Foundation was indeed resurrected by the reunited parishioners of *St. Jean Bosco* on the site of the old *Lafanmi Selavi* Bakery which was burned down by the military during the *coup d'e-tat*. Today it is a great meeting place which receives literally thousands of people each week.

Our home was also resurrected. I first came to the place I now live in 1988, after our church was burned. Then the land was covered with sugar cane; there were only a few trees. The people called my house a presbytery. It was then that I began planning to build the popular university with the poor with whom we worked. Two years later the house, like myself, had a dramatic change of role. In 1991 it served as the president's house, but it remained open to the poor. The night of the coup it was there that the soldiers came looking for me. The house was burned and gutted. In an act of bravery I will never forget, after the soldiers left, the people in the area rescued my books. Three years later, when I returned from exile, they brought them back to me.

Today we are close to creating that university and the house is at the service of so many people. The kids of *Lafanmi Selavi* have their agricultural projects here, they work, they learn and they play. From early in the morning to late at night we receive all kinds of people: members of popular organizations, groups from the countryside, priests, nuns, bishops, ambassadors, diplomats, politicians, both opponents and members of *Fanmi Lavalas*, foreigners and Haitians, members of the wealthiest families and the poorest. Among those I have received are those who financed the *coup d'etat*—those who paid, more than once, to have me killed. I have met with them not just once, but whenever it is necessary. If we do not yet have justice for the crimes of the coup, at least we find a little piece of justice in that we receive them on the same couches that welcome street children. These couches receive presidents, first ladies and *restaveks*, the Secretary General of the United Nations and our neighbor who sells bread on the street. Beyond class, beyond color is the human being. Our faith asks that whenever and with whomever we can address the issues that affect the poorest we cross borders and open dialogue.

Today the mango trees I planted ten years ago in the sugar cane fields give fruit and shade for our many visitors. The one thousand coconut trees we planted with the kids last year will bear fruit in four years, fruit that the students of the university will eat. In this same way we look forward to harvesting the fruits of dialogue and education that we plant today. Peace of stomach, and peace of mind.

Our world is facing profound economic and ecological questions. These experiences demonstrate that the answers we need may be theological ones.

God said to Moses, "I see the suffering of Israel; I hear the cry of the people." Do we? Do we hear God speaking through the poor? In a world oriented only toward profit, it may be difficult for us to hear God's voice above the din and the racket of the money-changers who have filled the world's temples. But God is not the market. God is love. God is justice. God is peace.

God is also a woman.

Wherever women are heard and respected, the face of God is illuminated. Wherever the poor are heard and respected, the face of God is illuminated. The gift of Christ is his humanity, his presence among the living, among the poor. Jesus is not only the God of glory; he is the God of suffering. He is quiet dignity in the face of misery, children who still smile, mothers who give love even when there is no food, the capacity to see hope through excruciating pain, acts of courage in the face of violence, determination in the face of impunity

Last year I met an extraordinary and yet ordinary Haitian man. His son was born on June 13, 1993, at a time when bodies were found on the streets of *Port-au-Prince* each morning, when mentioning the name Aristide was enough to get you killed. He went to the registrar in downtown *Port-au-Prince* and told the clerk to write the child's name on the birth certificate: Jean-Bertrand Aristide Riché. The clerk, seized with terror, said, "Are you crazy? Be quiet. They will kill you." The man insisted, offering to pay a small bribe. Finally he gave 50 gourdes and he got the birth certificate. Last year during a meeting at our Foundation, this man stood up and showed the crowd this same birth certificate. A badge of honor. Evidence that all the brutality the coup leaders could unleash on the country did not bring him to despair, that in the darkest moments the people create signs of light which sustain them.

This too is God's presence among us. God does not wait for us to build a peaceful and just world, but is present with us along the way, in the struggle, accompanying our pilgrimage, allowing us to feel joy throughout our journey.

Photo by Jennifer Cheek Pantaléon

Chapter Nine

The Challenge of 2004

During the coup, while I was in exile, a member of our parliament who was fiercely opposed to our return declared on television that I would never return. "The people should stop talking about Aristide," he said, "for when did you ever see an egg laid by a chicken go back into the chicken?" After my return, the people painted murals on walls throughout the country: a huge chicken, a huge egg, and a finger pushing the egg back into the chicken.

The year 2004 will mark two hundred years of Haitian independence. Can we achieve cultural, economic, and political independence by 2004? Can we put the egg back in the chicken again?

Long before 1804, from the moment they were taken from their homes, our ancestors began the struggle against slavery. How many millions rejected slavery by throwing themselves into the sea as the ships carried them from Africa? How many thousands poisoned themselves or their children rather than live as slaves? The revolution when it began took thirteen long years to achieve. Today, the weapons may be different, but we are in a similar moment of struggle, striving to realize 2004.

If 2004 represents a profound challenge to all Haitians, the turn of the century should represent a similar challenge for the world. Can we create a more just global economic order, can we tackle the inequalities that mark our age? Can we put that egg back into the chicken too?

Part of this challenge involves dramatically changing global spending priorities, which are so grotesquely skewed. It is estimated that only 10% of development aid goes towards meeting primary human needs (education, health care, clean water, and sanitation). This amount represents less than what the industrialized world spends on athletic shoes each year. It would take six billion dollars a year, for three years, in addition to what is already spent, to put every child in the world in school. Does this seem like a lot? It represents less than 1% of world military spending.

The United Nations Human Development Report for 1997 told us that poverty is no longer inevitable. The world has the material and natural resources, the know-how and people to make a poverty-free world a reality in less than a generation. "The time has come to create a world that is more human, more stable, more just. Eradicating poverty everywhere is more than a moral imperative and a commitment to human solidarity. It is a practical possibility. The costs of eradicating poverty are less than people imagine—

about 1% of global income and no more than 2–3% of national income in all but the poorest nations."

So it is possible. But one thing is certain, to get there we will have to take risks. We will have to assume them. And to assume risks requires faith. If you cannot cross the visible to what you cannot yet see, you will be stuck in doubts, pessimism, and defeatism. Faith arms you to believe and to assume risks.

During the period immediately following my return to Haiti in 1994, the most pressing issue facing us was the army. This same army which had led the *coup d'etat*, which had brutalized the population for three years, which in fact had led every *coup d'etat* in Haitian history, and served as a structure of repression which allowed the status quo to exist, was still there. Everywhere we went people were calling for the army to be disbanded. This force of repression, which in the end acceded to the intervention of the international community without a fight, had no shred of credibility left among the people.

In 1995, in accordance with the wishes of the great majority of the Haitian people, and against the will of many in the international community, we disbanded this military, reducing Haiti's military spending to zero. We did it step by step, over a period of months. On December 26, 1994 there was a kind of mutiny as the military, foreseeing the future, attacked the army headquarters demanding their pay. A foreign general came to see me. He threatened violence in no uncertain terms if we continued on this path.

But we continued, until February 1995, when the last soldiers were retired or transferred, or sent overseas. All that remained was the Palace Band. We bought them new instruments and new uniforms and made peace with them, too. The final step was to turn the military headquarters over to the newly-created Ministry of Women.

What had seemed impossible, unthinkable, only months before, was a reality. A break with 200 years of structural repression. An army, which had controlled 40% of the national budget, was no more.

The Haitian people reveled in their victory. Carnival in February 1995 was a kind of miracle. Millions poured out into the streets for a carnival without fear. There was no military; there was not yet a police; there was very little electricity. Yet with no force maintaining order other than the force of the people's will, this was one of the most peaceful carnivals in Haitian history.

We have a saying that "Haitians do not negotiate carnival," which is to say, we do not negotiate our culture. When a people dance and sing, they are not a hollow instrument. Rather their culture echoes through their voices and their bodies. They assume their roots, reaffirm themselves. In 1995, we celebrated the impossible.

One of the songs from carnival that year was "Zo Popey," which means literally "doll bones," referring to a dance style where you move as if you have no bones. This brings us to the last child in our story, a recent visitor to my home. On a day that we wel-

comed a group of *restaveks* to the house, five children who live in the streets with their grandmother,
sleeping on the steps of one of the churches of *Port-
au-Prince*, came to swim. The smallest was a beautiful, wild little thing, who acted as if no one had
raised her. Her name, she said, was Zo Popey.

Zo Popey must have been born during carnival of
1995, so she will be nine years old in 2004. Anatole
will be 30. Monique will be 20, Berthony 14,
Florence 13, Jean-Bertrand Aristide Riché will be 11
and Ti Moise will be eight years old. What will 2004
look like to them?

I see for them a country with 85% literacy, rather
than 85% illiteracy. Cooperatives flourish in villages
and in the informal sectors of the cities. Water is flow-
ing through the fields of the countryside—where food
enough for all of Haiti's people is growing. Creole pigs
are seen more and more in the countryside, the
descendents of those few that the peasants hid away
and saved from extermination. Seedlings are beginning to take root on the mountainsides. The seedlings
have a chance at survival because the people are no
longer in misery, but are already on the road to poverty with dignity. There are primary schools and health
clinics in every municipality of Haiti. The schoolbooks are not just half-price—they are free, in accordance with Article 32.1 of our constitution which
promises a free education to every Haitian child. The
children and young people are actively engaged in the
changes sweeping their country. *Radyo Timoun* can be
heard throughout the country, and people begin to

feel it is normal for children to have a voice in national issues. The *bayakou* and the *bouretye* still labor, but the weight of social exclusion has been lifted. The *restaveks* are eating at the table with everyone else.

This is our challenge for the new century; this is the challenge of 2004. We assume it. We are living it right now.

A lawyer who visited *Lafanmi Selavi* asked a boy what his future held. The child answered, "I am working so that all children in Haiti will have enough to eat." The statement was translated from Creole to French for the lawyer as "the boy wishes to see all children in Haiti have enough to eat." The child, understanding French as well as Creole, interrupted and quickly corrected the translation saying, "**Wishing** for children to have enough to eat implies that I am not working now, and that there is a chance that it may not come to pass. I want you to know that I am right now working so that all children in Haiti **will** have enough to eat."

To you, who read this book, we want you to know that we are right now working to realize the challenge of 2004 in Haiti. Our faith makes us certain it will come to pass. This faith, this certainty, may be the most valuable export we can offer the world. I invite you to share in it. You and I together, fingers of the same hand, are called to build a more human world in this new century, to bring the thumb and the little finger closer together, so the hand may be strong and whole. I am certain that we can and that we will.

Index

Index

Index

Photo by Alan Pogue

About the Author

On October 15, 1994, Jean-Bertrand Aristide returned to Haiti with the help of the United Nations to complete the remaining sixteen months of his presidential term. He had been forced into exile in 1991 during a military coup, after winning an overwhelming 67% majority of the vote in Haiti's first democratic presidential elections.

Aristide first came to prominence during the 1980s as an outspoken priest in one of the largest slums of *Port-au-Prince*, Haiti's capitol. His courageous criticism of the Duvalier regime, his message of hope to the Haitian people, and his affirmation of the dignity of each person regularly attracted thousands to his church. He soon became one of the best-known and most-loved leaders of Haiti's pro-democracy movement, which ultimately led to the fall of the 30-year dictatorship there.

Today, as an active former-head-of-state, Aristide remains profoundly committed to helping poor people in Haiti and around the world, often speaking out against the dangers of globalization and offering more just alternatives. He continues the work he began in the '80s through the Aristide Foundation for Democracy and *Lafanmi Selavi*, the center for street children he founded in 1986.

Proceeds from the sale of this book benefit the The Aristide Foundation for Democracy. The Foundation sponsors community-based economic projects, educational programs, and forums for dialogue aimed at giving a voice to those who have not traditionally had a voice in Haitian society. For more information on the Foundation, visit our website at www.FonAristide.org.

Tax deductible donations can be sent to:

The Aristide Foundation for Democracy
PO Box 409271
Miami, FL 33149